It's Our Business

Graphing

Harry James

Publishing Credits

Editor
Sara Johnson

Editorial Director
Dona Herweck Rice

Editor-in-Chief
Sharon Coan, M.S.Ed.

Creative Director
Lee Aucoin

Publisher
Rachelle Cracchiolo, M.S.Ed.

Image Credits

The author and publisher would like to gratefully credit or acknowledge the following for permission to reproduce copyright material: cover Shutterstock (all images); p.1 Shutterstock/Philip Hunton; p.4 bottom Getty images/L Klove,Photo service; p.4 top Shutterstock; p.6 Istock/S Dominick; p.9 Shutterstock/R.Gino Santa Maria; p.12 Getty images/B Langrish; p.16 Phototlibrary/Juniors Bildarchiv; p.18 bottom Shutterstock/G Victoria; p.18 top Pearson Education Australia/A McBroom; p.19 Photolibrary/C McKeone; p.20 Getty Images/K Hatsuzawa Neovision; p.23 top Shutterstock/E Isseleé; p.23 bottom Shutterstock/L Fernada Gonzalez; p.25 Photodisc vol 15; p.27 Alamy/Mindset Photography.

Teacher Created Materials
5301 Oceanus Drive
Huntington Beach, CA 92649-1030
http://www.tcmpub.com

ISBN 978-0-7439-0924-2

Reprinted 2013

Table of Contents

Animals on Our Minds

My name is Alex and my friends are Chen, Ari, and Karla. Last year, we started our own business. We wanted to earn extra money after school and during our vacations. Our business helps people look after their animals. We do jobs like walking dogs, feeding animals, cleaning cages and fish tanks, and grooming. Our business is called "Animals on Our Minds."

Our business started slowly. We did not have many jobs during the first few months. But soon the people we had helped told others about what we did. Then, our business began to grow. Lots of people got to know about us because we did a good job.

LET'S EXPLORE MATH

A graph is a kind of picture. It **visually** shows the **data**. A bar graph is a good way to **compare** data. This bar graph shows the number of hours the children spend in 1 week doing different jobs.

Hours Spent Doing Jobs

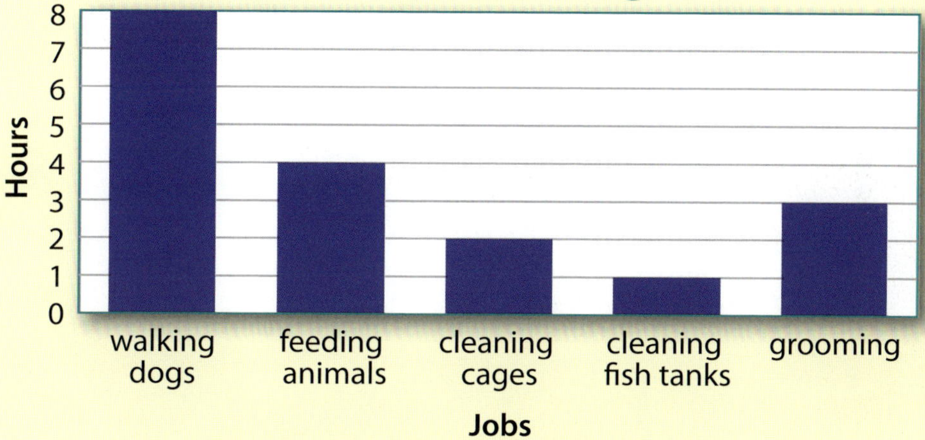

a. How many hours are spent walking dogs?

b. Which 2 tasks do the children spend the least amounts of time doing?

c. Which task do the children spend 3 hours per week doing?

Knowing Our Business

Karla's mom is an **accountant** (uh-KOWN-tuhnt). She helps people run their businesses. She helps people keep track of their **incomes** and **expenses**. We thought Karla's mom might be able to help with our business, too. So we asked her to come to a business meeting.

Karla's mom asked us questions like these: What jobs do you earn the most money doing? Are there other jobs you could be doing? Do you need to cut down how much money you spend? We were not sure of the answers. Karla's mom said she could help us.

Starting Young

Many young people turn their hobbies into businesses. They might make jewelry or sell lemonade. Do you have a hobby that you could turn into a business?

We decided to keep a notebook about our work. We wrote down all the jobs we have done since we started our business. We also wrote how much money we got paid and what we spent. Karla's mom told us that we could use this information to find out more about our business.

Animals on Our Minds — Job Notebook

February — Week 1

Mon. — washed Mrs. Henderson's dog, Flo (First Avenue)	$6.00
Tues. — walked Mr. Jackson's 2 dogs, Roger and Dodger (City Park)	$7.00
Wed. — fed Aunty Lucia's cat, Fluffy (Second Avenue)	$4.00
Thurs. — bought dog treats	– $6.50
Fri. — bought plastic dog brush	– $2.00
Sat. — fed Nanna Jones's cat for a week (Hilltop Street)	$28.00

Earning Money

We used the data to figure out which jobs earned us the most money. Karla's mom made a circle graph on her computer to show us this information. A circle graph is a good way to compare parts that make up the whole. The whole is all the jobs we do to earn money. The parts show each different job. The biggest part shows us which job earned us the most money. The smallest part shows us which job earned us the least money.

How We Earned Money

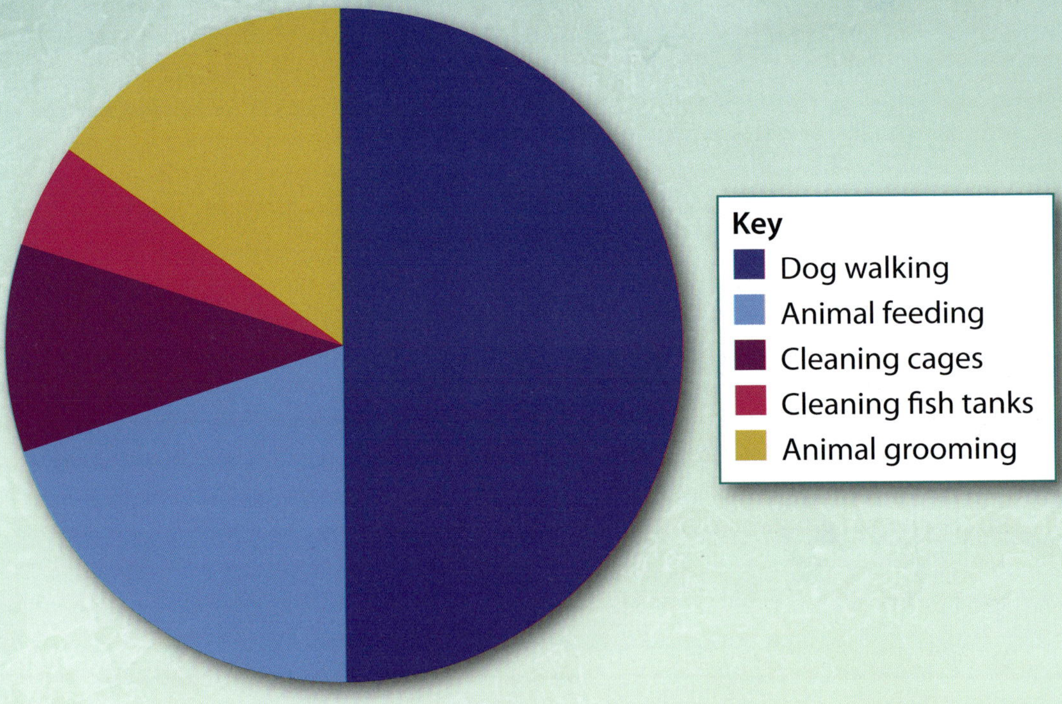

Most of our money came from walking dogs. This was not surprising. We had made ourselves T-shirts with our business name on them. People saw us out walking dogs in our T-shirts. They asked us if we could walk their dogs, too. We were like walking **advertisements** for our business!

LET'S EXPLORE MATH

Use the circle graph on page 8 to answer these questions.

a. Which job earns the most money? The least money?

b. Which job earns half of the money?

c. Which two jobs earn about the same amount of money?

We used other data to show us *when* we earned the most money. We made the most money during our summer vacation. That is when we have the most time to work. And people need someone to look after their animals when they are away on vacations.

We made this line graph to show the amount of money we earned during our first 6 months of business. Business was slow when we first started. We became busier after about 2 months.

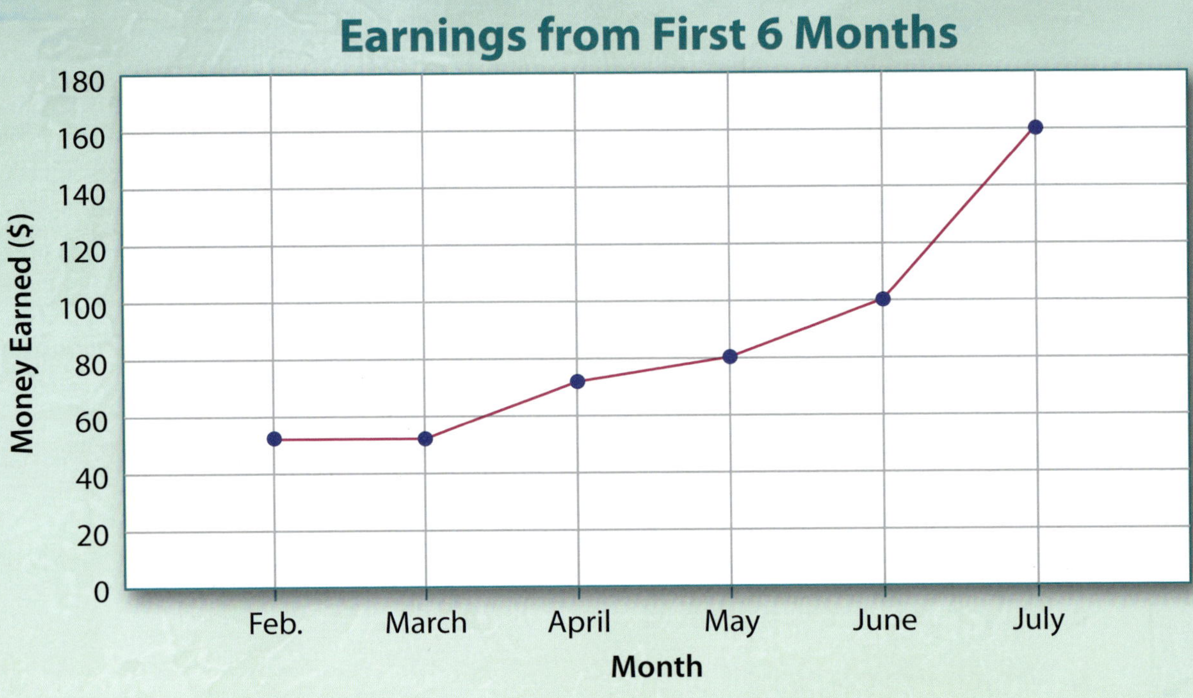

Spending Money

We kept a **record** of how much we had spent on the business. So Karla's mom made this circle graph to show our expenses. We spent most of our money on making posters and T-shirts. We bought a lot of dog treats as well!

Business Expenses

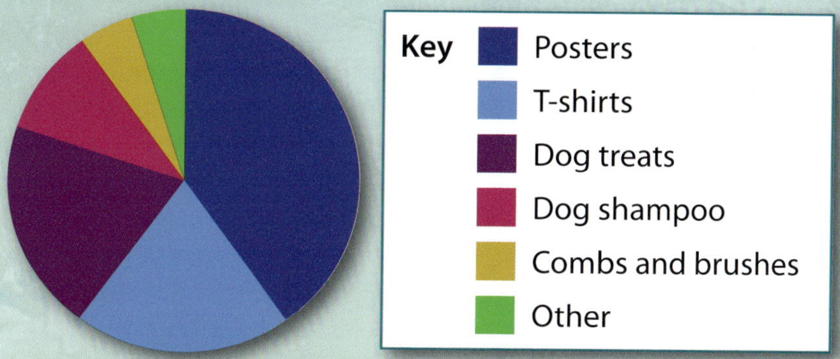

LET'S EXPLORE MATH

Line graphs are a good way to show data collected **continuously** over time. Use the line graph on page 10 to answer these questions.

a. In which months did the children earn the least money?

b. How much more money did the children earn in July than in May?

c. Based on the data, do you think the children will earn more or less in August than in July? Why?

The Survey

The data made us think about how our business could grow. There may be more jobs we could do to earn extra money. There may be more animals that we could look after.

I said we could help people train their puppies. We had never offered that before. Ari said we could clean more fishtanks. Karla said we could get some work at the local stables. She really likes horses, so that suggestion was no surprise!

Chen said we could ask people how we could help look after their animals. We thought this was a good idea. We wrote a list of questions for a **survey**. The answers could help us to make our business grow.

Survey Questions

1. Do you own an animal? yes / no

2. If yes, circle the animal(s) that you own:

   dog cat bird fish hamster rabbit

   other ____________ (State what type of animal.)

3. How many animals do you own? ____________

4. If you own a dog, which of these services would you use? (Circle your answer.)

dog walking dog grooming puppy training

Taking a Survey

We made 150 copies of the survey. Ari's dad took us to the local shopping mall. The mall was a good place to hold a survey. There are always lots of people shopping, and it is close to where we live. We also gave out **flyers** about our business. Lots of people took these flyers. We kept track of the number of people we surveyed, the number of people who have animals, and the number of people who took our flyers.

Most people were happy to complete our survey. We asked questions about the kinds of animals they have and how many. We also asked what **services** they might use. This included jobs we already did and new jobs we could do.

Data Gathered at the Mall

	Thursday	Friday	Saturday	Total
Number of people surveyed	37	44	58	139
Number of people who have animals	25	37	39	101
Number of people who took flyers	17	22	35	74

LET'S EXPLORE MATH

a. Use the information in the data table above to create a bar graph for the number of people surveyed, who have animals, or who took flyers. *Hint*: Don't forget to label the *x*-axis and the *y*-axis and give your graph a title.

b. Write 2 questions you could ask about the data found in your graph.

The Survey Results

There were 101 people who responded that they own animals. Chen typed the data into the computer. Most people had cats, dogs, birds, or fish. Some people had mice, rats, and rabbits. And others had spiders and snakes. These were part of the "Other" **category** in the survey. We made bar graphs to show our data.

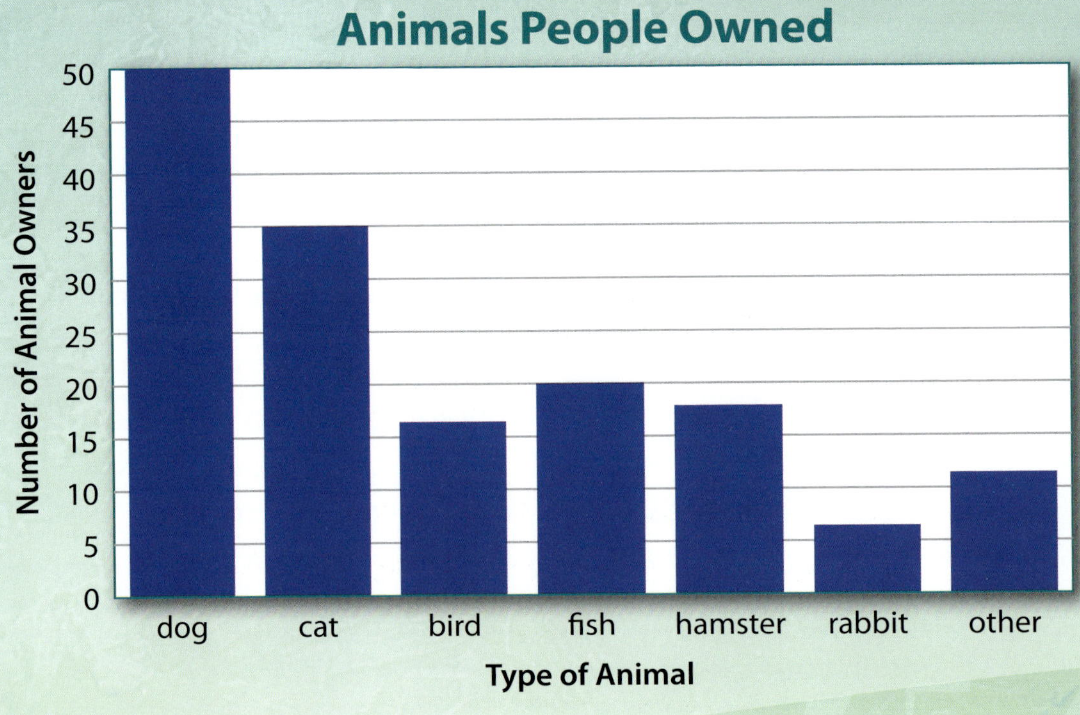

The data showed which animals were the most popular. It also showed how many animals of each type people had. There were many animals that we could help care for.

People Who Own Dogs

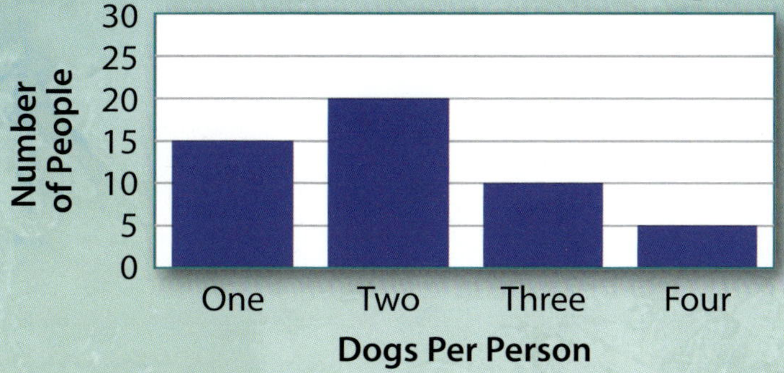

People Who Own Cats

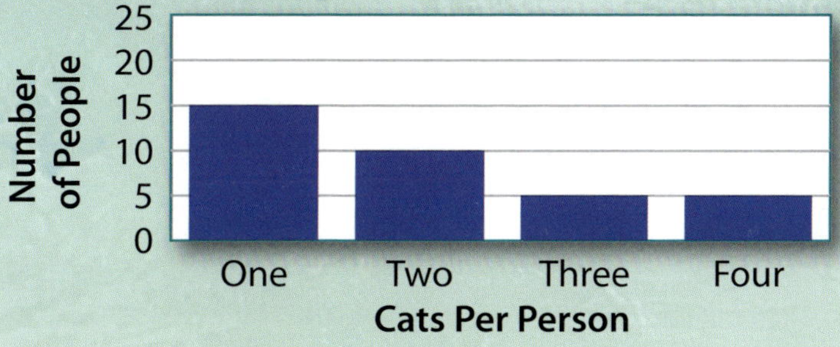

LET'S EXPLORE MATH

Use the graphs above to answer these questions.

a. How many people own 1 dog?

b. How many people own 2 cats?

c. How many more people had 2 dogs than 2 cats?

d. Do more people own dogs or cats?

The survey showed that our most popular service was dog walking. Grooming was popular, too. We want to do these jobs more often.

We need a cheaper way to buy shampoo and brushes. We decide to buy larger bottles of shampoo and better brushes. Larger shampoo bottles are much cheaper per wash than small ones. They last longer, too. Better brushes cost more, but they last longer than cheap ones. That means that we will buy fewer brushes over time.

The survey showed that our least popular service was cleaning fishtanks. However, many people own fish. So, we need to let more people know that we offer this service.

Finally, the survey helped us figure out which new services we could offer. Puppy training was very popular. So, we decided to offer that service as well.

LET'S EXPLORE MATH

Create a survey about the different types of pets your classmates own. Then make a bar graph using your data. *Hint*: Some of the survey questions on page 13 may help you get started.

Where Our Jobs Are Located

Chen talked about how our jobs seemed to be farther from home. On Saturday, she had taken 4 large dogs for a walk in Central Park. Chen felt like she was spending more time traveling to collect the dogs than walking them. We needed to know whether we were spending too much time traveling to jobs.

LET'S EXPLORE MATH

The table below shows the hours the children spent traveling for their business in 1 week.

Children	Hours Spent Traveling
Alex	4
Ari	3
Karla	5
Chen	4

a. Graph the data using a graph of your choice.

b. Explain why you chose that type of graph.

We always write down the address for each job. So we decided to compare where our jobs were in the first 3 months and the most recent 3 months of the business. We used a map and colored pins to help us.

First, Chen read out the **locations** for all the jobs in the first 3 months. Ari put red pins in the map at those places.

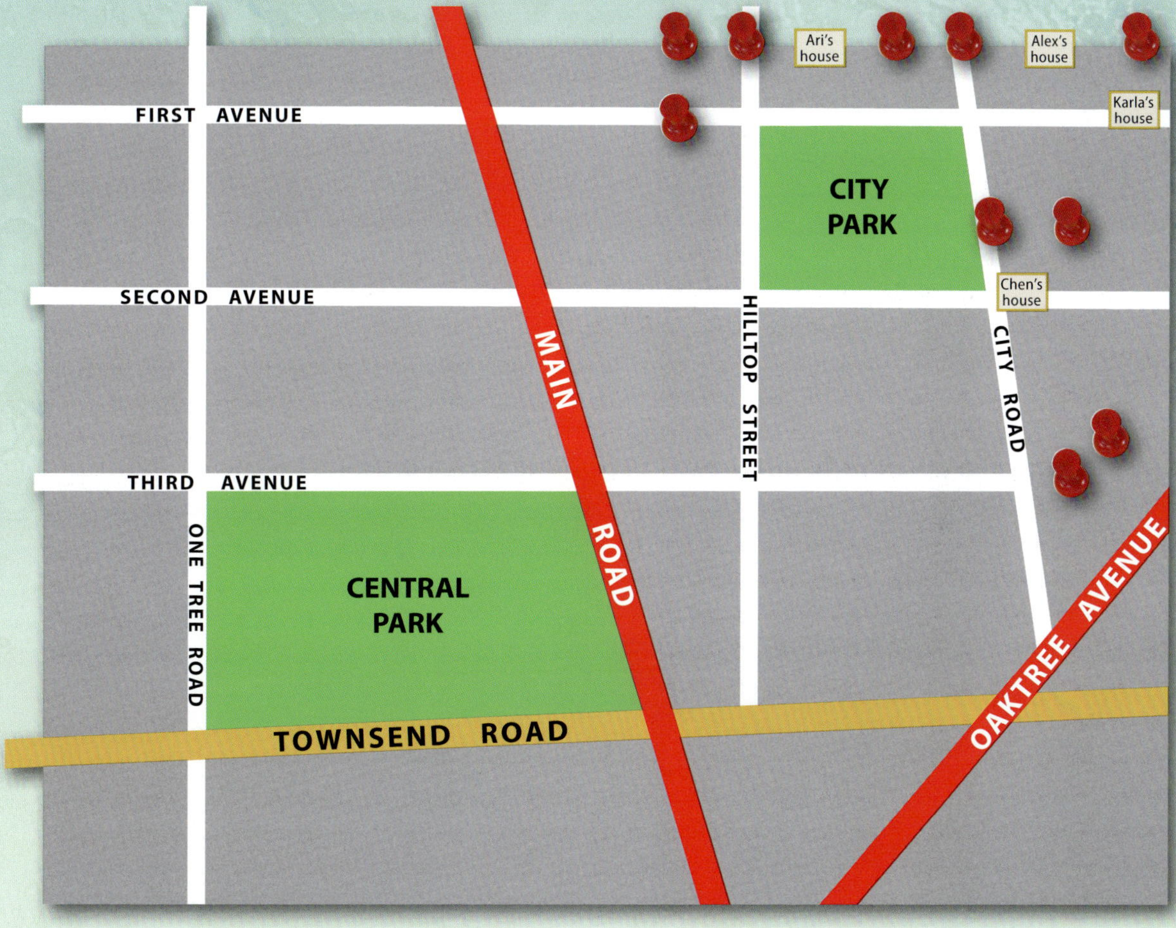

Then Chen read out all the locations for jobs in the most recent 3 months. Ari put blue pins on the map to show those places. There were more blue pins than red pins on the map. The blue pins were farther from where we lived, too. It was easy to see that we were doing more jobs in the last 3 months, and these jobs were often farther away.

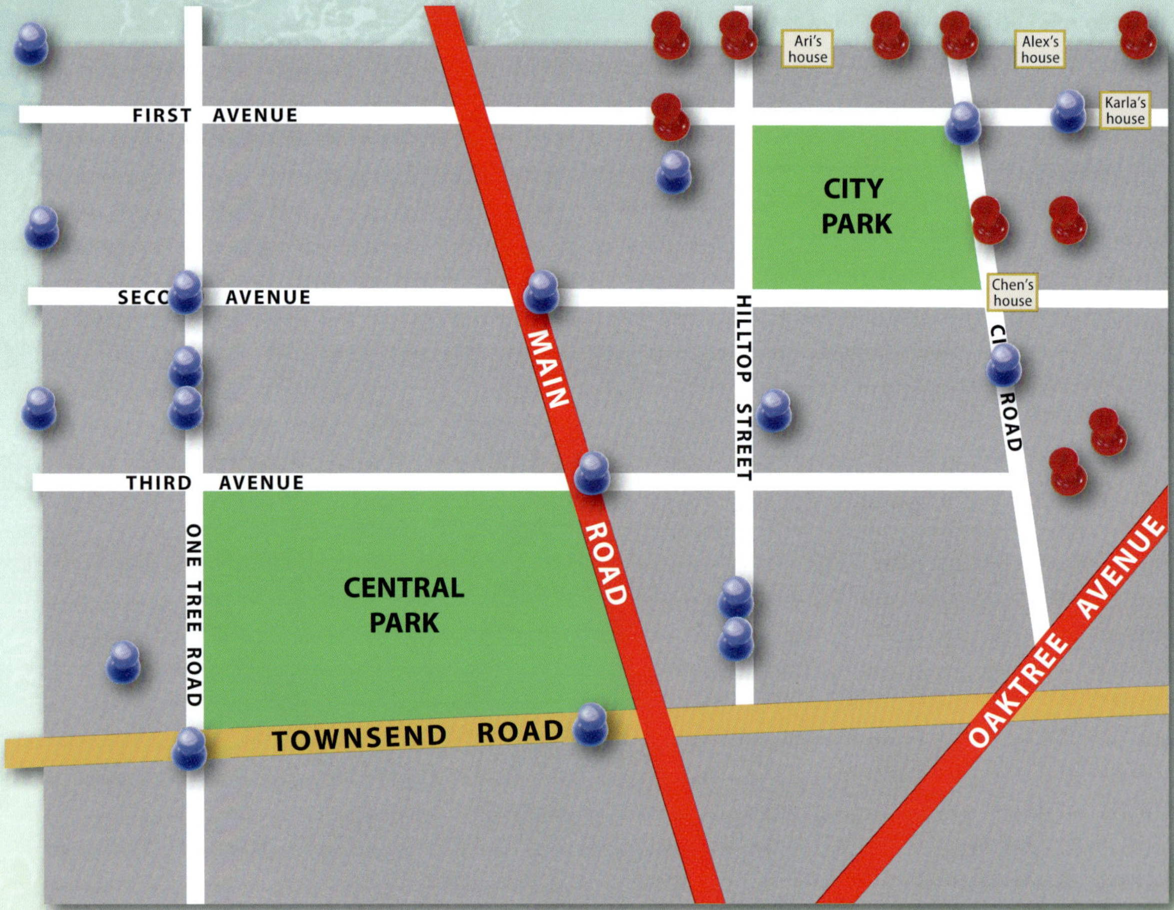

We showed the map to Karla's mom. We told her about jobs that we had not been able to do. We were too busy traveling or doing other jobs. Karla's mom suggested that we get more kids to work for the business. We had never thought about that.

Sometimes, we had to say "No" when people asked us to walk dogs. We had no time.

Cleaning birdcages was a popular service, but we did not always have time to do it.

More Kids?

Mrs. Lee, one of our best customers, asked us to wash her dog the next day. But we all had other jobs on that afternoon.

That night, Karla's mom made us a double bar graph. It showed the jobs we did in the last week. It also showed the jobs that we did not do because we did not have time.

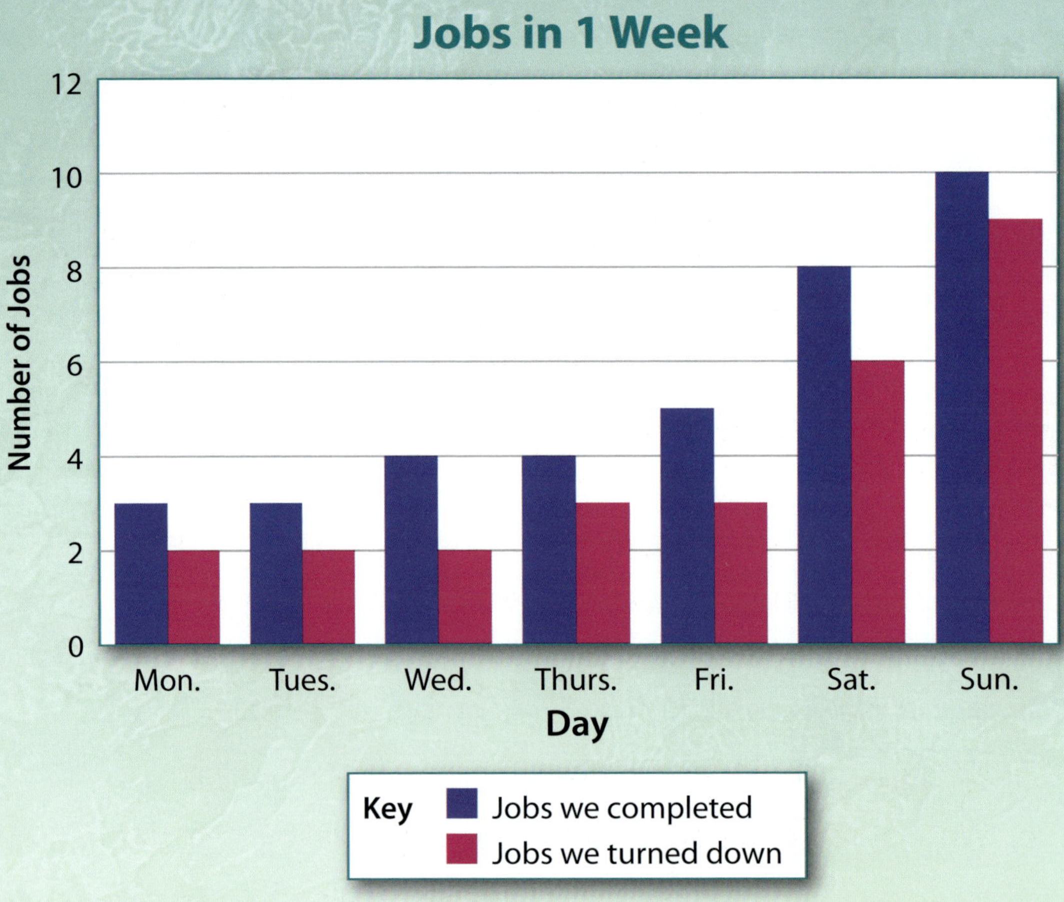

We asked Ari's sister, Talia, to help us wash Mrs. Lee's dog the next afternoon. Talia enjoyed the job. We asked if she would like to work in our business. Talia said yes. The next time there was a job and we were all busy, we would ask Talia to help. Our business really was growing.

LET'S EXPLORE MATH

The double bar graph on page 24 compares 2 sets of data on the same graph. It is easy to see what is the same and what is different. Use the graph to answer these questions:

a. How many jobs were turned down on Saturday?

b. How many jobs were offered in total on Wednesday?

c. Write at least one observation about the data in the graph.

d. Write a question that can be answered using the information in the graph.

A Growing Business

Months later, we made another circle graph comparing the money we earned from different jobs. This time, the circle graph included some new services. We still earn the most money from dog walking. And our cleaning fish tank service now makes up a greater fraction of the whole circle.

We when looked at all our data, we **concluded** that the survey and new flyers were worth the effort!

How We Earned Money

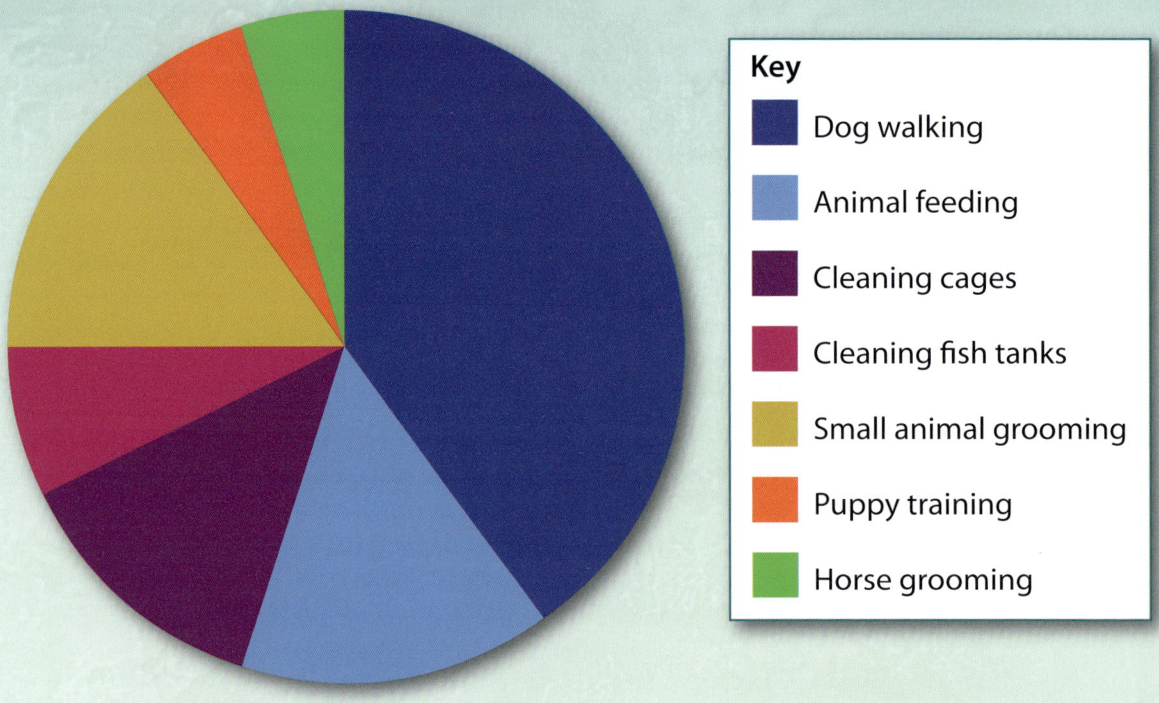

Our business now offers 2 more services than when we first started. What will this circle graph look like next summer?

If our business keeps growing, we will have to hire 2 more kids by the end of the school year. They can help us during summer vacation. Next summer, "Animals on Our Minds" will be looking after nearly all the animals in town!

PROBLEM-SOLVING ACTIVITY

Surf's Up?

Emilio owns a small surfing goods store. He would like to expand his business. The store next door is available to rent. Emilio needs to find out if his business is growing to see if he can afford to expand.

Business expenses total $1,200 per month for 2008. Emilio creates a circle graph to show the percentage of different expenses.

Breakdown of Expenses

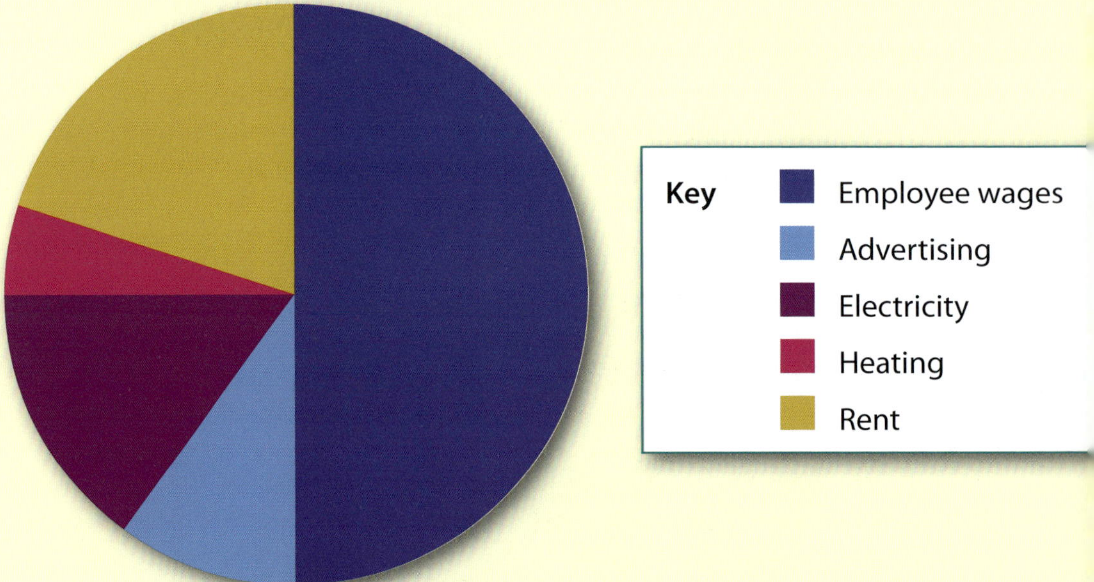

Emilio also makes a table to show his sales per month for the past year.

2008 Sales

Jan.	Feb.	Mar.	Apr.	May	June
$900	$900	$1,100	$1,400	$1,500	$1,800
July	**Aug.**	**Sept.**	**Oct.**	**Nov.**	**Dec.**
$2,000	$2,100	$1,700	$1,500	$1,300	$1,300

Solve It!

Use the circle graph on page 28 to figure out:

a. Which expense costs Emilio the most each month?

b. Which expense costs Emilio the least each month?

Now use the table above to complete these questions.

c. Create a bar graph to show the sales for 2008.

d. Do you think Emilio should expand his business? List your reasons.

Use the steps below to help you create your graph. Remember to label the axes and give your graph a title.

Step 1: First, decide what data in the table to use for the *x*-axis and *y*-axis.

Step 2: Now create your bar graph using the amounts in the table. Label the graph and give it a title.

Glossary

accountant—a person who records and monitors the money paid and received by a business or individual

advertisements—notices that tell people about a service or product

category—a group containing items of a similar type

compare—to look at the features of two or more things to see how they are the same or different

concluded—decided

continuously—nonstop; uninterrupted

data—information

expenses—things that people spend money on

flyers—advertising brochures

incomes—amounts of money earned

locations—places

record—a written note

services—jobs done for someone

survey—a list of questions used to find information

visually—as a picture, image, or display

Index

ANSWER KEY

Let's Explore Math

Page 5:

a. 8 hours

b. Cleaning fish tanks and cleaning cages

c. Grooming

Page 9:

a. Dog walking earns the most money. Cleaning fish tanks earns the least money.

b. Dog walking

c. Animal grooming and animal feeding

Page 11:

a. February and March

b. $80.00 more

c. Answers will vary but could include the fact they children will probably earn more money in August, given that the data shows that they earned more in the summer months. August is also when the children are on school vacation and have more time to work.

Page 15:

a. Answers will vary.

b. Answers will vary.

Page 17:

a. 15 people

b. 10 people

c. 10 more people

d. More people own dogs than cats.

Page 19:

Answers will vary.

Page 20:

Answers will vary.

Page 25:

a. 6 jobs

b. 6 jobs

c. Answers will vary but could include the fact that the data shows that the children complete the most number of jobs on the weekend.

d. Answers will vary.

Problem-Solving Activity

a. Employee wages

b. Heating

c.

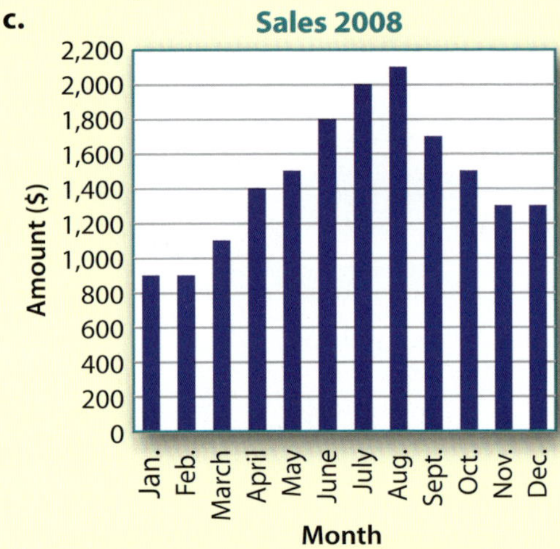

d. Answers may vary, but given that the bar graph shows that Emilio is making more sales and is meeting his expenses, he could afford to expand his business.